You Must Be Born Again, or,
Because of Media and Entertainment,
Every Person is an Actor.

Apostle Bill Amor

"You Must Be Born Again, or, Because of Media and Entertainment, Every Person is an Actor"
written by Bill Amor
1st Edition © 2025 by Bill Amor
ISBN: 979-8-9995696-4-6

Contents

CONTENTS

Summary for Apostle Bill Amor's Book

"You Must Be Born Again, or, Because of Media and Entertainment, Every Person is an Actor" explores the profound biblical truth that spiritual rebirth is essential for entering God's kingdom (John 3:3). Drawing from Scripture, Apostle Bill Amor examines how modern media and entertainment have turned society into a stage where individuals often play roles dictated by cultural expectations rather than living authentically in Christ.

The book begins by unpacking Jesus' conversation with Nicodemus in John 3, emphasizing that being 'born again' is not merely a religious phrase but a transformative experience through water and Spirit (John 3:5). Without this new birth, individuals remain spiritually blind to God's kingdom realities.

Apostle Amor then delves into how media and entertainment perpetuate superficial identities, likening them to masks worn by actors on a stage. Referencing Romans 12:2, he challenges readers not to conform to worldly patterns but instead embrace renewal through Christ. He warns against serving two masters (Matthew 6:24), urging believers to reject false personas crafted by societal pressures and instead live as new creations in Christ (2 Corinthians 5:17).

Through compelling insights and scriptural analysis, this book calls readers to examine their lives critically—are they merely acting out roles imposed by culture, or are they truly born again? With practical guid-

ance rooted in biblical doctrine, Apostle Amor inspires believers to shed worldly facades and pursue genuine transformation through faith in Jesus Christ.

Chapter 1: The Necessity of Being Born Again

This chapter introduces the foundational concept of being "born again," as taught by Jesus in John 3:3-7. It explains why spiritual rebirth is essential for entering the Kingdom of God. The chapter also contrasts physical birth with spiritual birth and sets the stage for understanding how worldly influences can hinder this transformation.

Key Scripture: *"Jesus answered and said unto him, Verily, verily, I say unto thee, Except a man be born again, he cannot see the kingdom of God."* (John 3:3)

Chapter 2: The Deception of Media and Entertainment

This chapter explores how modern media and entertainment shape perceptions, values, and behaviors. Drawing from biblical warnings about deception (Matthew 24:4), it discusses how these influences can lead individuals away from truth and authenticity.

Key Scripture: *"And Jesus answered and said unto them, Take heed that no man deceive you."* (Matthew 24:4)

Chapter 3: Every Person as an Actor

Using Romans 12:2 as a foundation, this chapter examines how societal pressures encourage people to "perform" rather than live authentically. It highlights how individuals often conform to roles dictated by culture rather than seeking God's purpose for their lives.

Key Scripture: *"And be not conformed to this world: but be ye transformed by the renewing of your mind..."* (Romans 12:2)

Chapter 4: The Role of Sin in Human Performance

This chapter delves into the biblical concept of sin as a driving force behind human pretense. Referencing Romans 3:23, it explains how sin separates humanity from God and leads people to wear masks to hide their brokenness.

Key Scripture: *"For all have sinned, and come short of the glory of God;"* (Romans 3:23)

Chapter 5: Jesus Christ – The True Light

Here, Apostle Bill Amor emphasizes Jesus as the ultimate source of truth who exposes falsehoods perpetuated by worldly systems. This chapter draws from John 8:12 to show how walking in Christ's light reveals our true identity.

Key Scripture: *"Then spake Jesus again unto them, saying, I am the light of the world..."* (John 8:12)

Chapter 6: Transformation Through Repentance

This chapter focuses on repentance as a critical step toward being born again. Using Acts 3:19 as a guide, it explains how turning away from sin allows individuals to experience spiritual renewal.

Key Scripture: *"Repent ye therefore, and be converted..."* (Acts 3:19)

Chapter 7: Casting Off Old Roles

Drawing from Ephesians 4:22-24, this chapter encourages readers to abandon their old selves—symbolized by roles they have played—and embrace their new identity in Christ.

Key Scripture: *"...put off concerning the former conversation the old man... And that ye put on the new man..."* (Ephesians 4:22-24)

Chapter 8: Renewing Your Mind Through God's Word

This chapter emphasizes studying scripture as a means to renew one's mind and resist worldly influences. Psalm 119 serves as a key reference for understanding how God's Word provides guidance.

Key Scripture:*"Thy word is a lamp unto my feet..."* (Psalm 119:105)

Chapter 9: Walking in Truth Amidst Deception

Using John 17:17 as its foundation, this chapter teaches readers how to live authentically in a world filled with lies. It stresses sanctification through truth found in God's Word.

Key Scripture:*"Sanctify them through thy truth..."* (John17;17)

Chapter 1: The Necessity of Being Born Again

Introduction: The Foundational Teaching of Spiritual Rebirth

The concept of being "born again" is one of the most profound and essential teachings in the Bible. It is introduced by Jesus Christ during His conversation with Nicodemus, a Pharisee and ruler of the Jews, as recorded in John 3:3-7. This teaching forms the cornerstone of Christian faith and salvation, emphasizing that no one can enter or even see the Kingdom of God without experiencing spiritual rebirth.

In John 3:3, Jesus declares, **"Verily, verily, I say unto thee, Except a man be born again, he cannot see the kingdom of God."** This statement underscores the absolute necessity of being born again—not as an optional step but as a requirement for eternal life. In this chapter, we will explore what it means to be born again, why it is necessary for salvation, and how worldly influences can obstruct this transformative process.

Understanding Spiritual Rebirth

To fully grasp the necessity of being born again, it is important to understand what Jesus meant by this term. When Nicodemus heard Jesus' words in John 3:4—**"How can a man be born when he is old? Can he enter the second time into his mother's womb and be born?"**—he was perplexed because he interpreted Jesus' statement literally. However, Jesus clarified in John 3:5-6: **"Except a man be born of water and of the Spirit, he cannot enter into**

the kingdom of God. That which is born of the flesh is flesh; and that which is born of the Spirit is spirit."

Here, Jesus distinguishes between two types of birth:

1. **Physical Birth (Born of Flesh):** This refers to our natural birth into this world through our parents. It represents our physical existence but does not grant us access to God›s Kingdom.

2. **Spiritual Birth (Born of Spirit):** This refers to a supernatural transformation brought about by the Holy Spirit. It involves a renewal of our inner being—a complete change in our heart and mind— that aligns us with God›s will.

Spiritual rebirth is not something we can achieve through human effort or good works; it is entirely dependent on God's grace and power working within us.

Why Is Being Born Again Necessary?

1. The Fallenness of Humanity

The Bible teaches that all humans are born into sin due to Adam's disobedience (Romans 5:12). As descendants of Adam, we inherit a sinful nature that separates us from God. Isaiah 64:6 states that even our righteous deeds are like "filthy rags" before Him because they are tainted by sin.

Without spiritual rebirth, we remain spiritually dead—alienated from God and incapable of pleasing Him (Ephesians

2:1-3). Being born again restores our relationship with God by cleansing us from sin and imparting new life through Christ.

2. Entrance Into God's Kingdom

Jesus explicitly states in John 3:3 that no one can "see" or "enter" the Kingdom of God without being born again. The Kingdom represents both God's rule over His people now and His eternal reign in heaven. To participate in this Kingdom requires more than external conformity to religious practices; it demands an inward transformation that only comes through spiritual rebirth.

3. Becoming Children of God

Through spiritual rebirth, we become children of God—a privilege granted only to those who receive Christ by faith (John 1:12-13). This new identity enables us to live as heirs to God's promises and reflect His character in our lives.

Contrasting Physical Birth With Spiritual Birth

Physical birth brings us into this world as partakers in human life but leaves us spiritually disconnected from God due to sin. In contrast:

- **Physical Birth:** Limited to earthly existence; bound by mortality.

- **Spiritual Birth:** Opens the door to eternal life; connects us with God›s divine nature (2 Peter 1:4).

While physical birth equips us for temporal living on earth, spiritual birth prepares us for eternal fellowship with God in heaven.

Worldly Influences That Hinder Spiritual Rebirth

In today's world dominated by media and entertainment, many individuals are distracted from seeking spiritual truth. These influences often promote values contrary to biblical principles—such as materialism, self-indulgence, and moral relativism—which can harden hearts against God's call for repentance.

Paul warns in Romans 12:2: **"And be not conformed to this world: but be ye transformed by the renewing of your mind..."** Conformity to worldly patterns prevents individuals from recognizing their need for spiritual renewal. Instead, believers must resist these influences by focusing on God›s Word and allowing His Spirit to work within them.

Conclusion

Being "born again" is not merely a religious phrase or abstract concept—it is an essential reality for anyone who desires to see or enter the Kingdom of God. As Jesus explained to Nicodemus in John 3:7—**"Marvel not that I said unto thee, Ye must be born again."**

This chapter has laid the foundation for understanding why spiritual rebirth is necessary for salvation and how it differs from physical birth. In subsequent chapters, we will delve deeper into how individuals can experience this transformation through repentance, faith in Christ, and reliance on the Holy Spirit while navigating challenges posed by worldly influences.

Key Scripture Recap: **"Jesus answered and said unto him, Verily, verily, I say unto thee, Except a man be born again, he cannot see the kingdom of God." (John 3:3)**

Chapter 2: The Deception of Media and Entertainment

Introduction: A World of Influence

In today's world, media and entertainment have become some of the most powerful forces shaping human thought, behavior, and values. From television shows to social media platforms, movies to music, these mediums have an unparalleled ability to influence how people perceive themselves, others, and the world around them. While technology and creativity can be used for good, the Bible warns us about the dangers of deception. Jesus Himself cautioned His followers in Matthew 24:4: **"And Jesus answered and said unto them, Take heed that no man deceive you."** This warning is as relevant today as it was two thousand years ago because deception has taken on new forms through modern media.

This chapter will explore how media and entertainment often distort truth, promote ungodly values, and encourage individuals to live inauthentic lives. By understanding these influences through a biblical lens, believers can guard their hearts and minds against deception.

The Power of Media to Shape Perceptions

Media has an extraordinary ability to shape perceptions by presenting curated narratives that may not reflect reality. News outlets often prioritize sensationalism over truth; social media platforms showcase idealized versions of life; movies and television frequently glorify sin while trivializing righteousness. These portrayals can lead individuals to adopt distorted views of what is normal or desirable.

The Bible reminds us in Isaiah 5:20: **"Woe unto them that call evil good, and good evil; that put darkness for light, and light for darkness; that put bitter for sweet, and sweet for bitter!"** Modern media often blurs the lines between good and evil by normalizing behaviors that contradict God's Word. For example:

- Immorality is glamorized in films.

- Greed is celebrated in reality TV shows.

- Violence is desensitized through video games.

These subtle yet pervasive messages can erode moral convictions over time if believers are not vigilant.

Entertainment as a Tool for Escapism

Entertainment offers an escape from reality—a temporary reprieve from life's challenges. While rest and recreation are not inherently wrong (Ecclesiastes 3:1), excessive indulgence in entertainment can distract individuals from their spiritual responsibilities. Many people turn to binge-watching series or scrolling endlessly on social media instead of spending time in prayer or studying God's Word.

Proverbs 4:23 warns us: **"Keep thy heart with all diligence; for out of it are the issues of life."** When we allow our hearts to be consumed by worldly entertainment rather than godly pursuits, we risk becoming spiritually complacent. Furthermore, escapism through entertainment often leads individuals to avoid confronting deeper issues such as sin or brokenness—issues that only Christ can heal.

The Subtle Nature of Deception

One of the most dangerous aspects of media-driven deception is its subtlety. Satan rarely presents lies outright; instead, he mixes falsehood with just enough truth to make it seem plausible. This tactic mirrors his approach in Genesis 3 when he deceived Eve by twisting God's words.

Modern media employs similar strategies:

1. **Relativism:** Promoting the idea that truth is subjective («What's true for you may not be true for me»).

2. **Desensitization:** Gradually normalizing sinful behaviors so they no longer seem shocking or wrong.

3. **Idolatry:** Encouraging people to idolize celebrities or material possessions rather than worshiping God.

Jesus warned about such deceptions when He said in John 8:44: **"Ye are of your father the devil...he is a liar, and the father of it."** Believers must remain discerning, so they do not fall prey to these tactics.

Living Authentically Amidst False Narratives

As Christians navigate a world saturated with deceptive messages from media and entertainment industries, they are called to live authentically according to God's truth rather than conforming to societal expectations (Romans 12:2). Authentic living requires:

- **Discernment:** Testing every message against Scripture (1 John 4:1).

- **Self-Control:** Limiting exposure to harmful content (Philippians 4:8).

- **Boldness:** Standing firm in faith even when it contradicts popular culture (Ephesians 6:13).

By anchoring their identity in Christ rather than seeking validation from likes or followers online (Galatians 1:10), believers can resist the pressure to "perform" for others' approval.

Conclusion: Taking Heed Against Deception

Jesus' warning in Matthew 24:4—**"Take heed that no man deceives you"**—is a call for vigilance in every area of life but especially regarding influences like media and entertainment. These tools have immense potential either to edify or corrupt depending on how they are used. As Apostle Bill Amor emphasizes throughout this book, being born again involves shedding old patterns shaped by worldly influences and embracing new life in Christ.

Believers must actively guard their hearts against deception by immersing themselves in God's Word daily (Psalm 119:11) while also encouraging others around them toward truthfulness over pretense. In doing so, they fulfill their role as "the light of the world" (Matthew 5:14), shining brightly amidst a culture darkened by falsehoods perpetuated through screens large and small.

Chapter 3: Every Person as an Actor

Key Scripture: *«And be not conformed to this world: but be ye transformed by the renewing of your mind, that ye may prove what is that good, and acceptable, and perfect, will of God.»* (Romans 12:2)

Introduction: The Stage of Life

In today's world, it often seems as though life itself has become a stage, with every person playing a role. From social media profiles carefully curated to project an ideal image to the expectations placed upon individuals by family, friends, and society at large, people are constantly performing. This chapter explores how societal pressures encourage individuals to conform to roles dictated by culture rather than living authentically in alignment with God's purpose. Drawing from Romans 12:2, we will examine how believers can resist these pressures and instead embrace transformation through the renewal of their minds.

The World's Script: Conformity and Performance

The Apostle Paul's admonition in Romans 12:2 begins with a clear command: *"Be not conformed to this world."* To conform means to shape oneself according to a pattern or mold. In the context of this verse, "the world" refers to the present age—its values, priorities, and systems that are often contrary to God's will.

Modern society provides countless scripts for how people should live their lives. These scripts dictate what success looks like, how relationships should function, what beauty entails, and even what beliefs are acceptable. Media and entertainment play a significant role in reinforcing these narratives. From reality television shows that glorify materialism to advertisements that prey on insecurities, the world encourages individuals to adopt roles that prioritize external appearances over internal truth.

This pressure to conform can lead people into a life of performance—acting out roles that please others or align with societal expectations but fail to reflect their true selves or God's design for them. For example:

- A young professional may feel compelled to pursue wealth and status at the expense of spiritual growth.

- A teenager might adopt behaviors or attitudes promoted by influencers on social media in order to fit in.

- Even within religious communities, there can be pressure to appear outwardly righteous while neglecting genuine faith and obedience.

Such conformity ultimately leads to emptiness because it is rooted in human approval rather than divine purpose.

The Danger of Wearing Masks

The Bible frequently warns against hypocrisy—pretending to be something one is not. Jesus rebuked the Pharisees for their outward displays of piety while their hearts were far from God (Matthew 23:27-28). Similarly, when individuals conform to worldly standards or play roles dictated by culture, they risk becoming actors who wear masks rather than living authentically.

This phenomenon is particularly evident in the age of social media. Platforms like Instagram and TikTok encourage users to present an idealized version of themselves—highlighting achievements while hiding struggles. While there is nothing inherently wrong with sharing positive moments, this constant performance can create a disconnect between one's public persona and private reality.

Moreover, wearing masks prevents genuine connection with others and with God. When people prioritize appearances over authenticity:

1. They may struggle with feelings of inadequacy or imposter syndrome because they know their public image does not reflect their true self.

2. They miss opportunities for meaningful relationships based on vulnerability and honesty.

3. They hinder spiritual growth by focusing on external validation rather than seeking God's approval.

Transformation Through Renewal

Paul contrasts conformity with transformation—a complete change from within brought about by the renewing of one's mind. This renewal involves aligning one's thoughts, values, and priorities with God's Word rather than the world's standards.

To experience this transformation:

1. **Immerse Yourself in Scripture:** The Bible serves as a guide for understanding God's will and discerning truth from deception (Psalm 119:105). Regular study allows believers to identify areas where they have conformed to worldly patterns and replace those influences with biblical principles.

2. **Pray for Wisdom:** James 1:5 promises that God gives wisdom generously to those who ask Him. Prayer helps believers seek guidance in navigating cultural pressures while remaining faithful.

3. **Surround Yourself with Godly Influences:** Proverbs 13:20 reminds us that *"He that walketh with wise men shall be wise."* Fellowship with other believers provides encouragement and accountability in resisting conformity.

4. **Focus on Eternal Rewards:** Colossians 3:2 urges Christians to *"Set your affection on things above..."* By prioritizing eternal values over temporary gains, believers can resist the temptation to perform for worldly approval.

Living Authentically in Christ

When individuals embrace transformation through Christ, they no longer need to act out roles dictated by culture or seek validation from others. Instead:

- They find their identity in being children of God (John 1:12).

- They live according to His purpose rather than societal expectations (Jeremiah 29:11).

- They experience freedom from the burden of performance because they rest in His grace (Ephesians 2:8-9).

Living authentically does not mean abandoning all responsibilities or ignoring cultural norms entirely; rather, it means approaching every aspect of life—from work and relationships to leisure activities—with integrity rooted in faith.

Conclusion: Proving God's Will

Paul concludes Romans 12:2 by stating that transformation enables believers to *"prove what is that good, and acceptable, and perfect will of God."* When Christians resist conformity and embrace renewal through Christ:

1. Their lives become testimonies of His goodness.

2. They demonstrate what it means to live authentically according to His design.

3. They fulfill their unique role in advancing His Kingdom—not as actors playing parts but as redeemed individuals walking in truth.

In a world obsessed with appearances and performances, choosing authenticity requires courage—but it also brings unparalleled freedom and joy found only in Christ Jesus.

Chapter 4: The Role of Sin in Human Performance

Sin, as described in the Bible, is a universal condition that affects every human being. It is not merely an act of wrong-doing but a state of separation from God—a spiritual chasm that distorts our identity and purpose. In this chapter, we will explore how sin acts as a driving force behind human pretense, compelling individuals to wear masks and play roles that conceal their true selves. By examining the bibli-cal concept of sin through the lens of Romans 3:23—"For all have sinned and come short of the glory of God"—we will uncover how this separation from God's glory leads to a life of performance rather than authenticity.

The Universality of Sin

The Apostle Paul makes it clear in Romans 3:23 that sin is a universal reality: "For all have sinned." This statement leaves no room for exceptions; every person, regardless of status, culture, or background, has fallen short of God's perfect standard. Sin is not just about individual actions but about a deeper condition inherited from humanity's first dis-obedience in the Garden of Eden (Genesis 3). This inherent sin nature creates a barrier between humanity and God, leaving people spiritually lost and searching for meaning.

This separation from God manifests itself in various ways, one of which is the tendency to hide our flaws and weak-nesses. Just as Adam and Eve covered themselves with fig leaves after their disobedience (Genesis 3:7), humans today often use metaphorical masks to cover their brokenness. These masks are shaped by societal expectations, personal insecurities, and the desire to appear righteous or successful in the eyes of others.

Sin as the Root Cause of Pretense

At its core, sin drives people to live inauthentically. Instead of embracing their true identity as beings created in God's image (Genesis 1:27), individuals often conform to roles dictated by worldly standards. This performance-driven mindset stems from the fear of rejection or judgment—a fear rooted in humanity's awareness of its own imperfection.

Consider how Jesus addressed the Pharisees in Matthew 23:27-28: "Woe unto you, scribes and Pharisees, hypocrites! for ye are like unto whited sepulchres, which indeed appear beautiful outwardly, but are within full of dead men's bones." Here, Jesus exposes the hypocrisy of religious leaders who prioritized outward appearances over inward transformation. Their behavior illustrates how sin compels people to focus on external performance while neglecting the condition of their hearts.

In modern times, this tendency is amplified by cultural influences such as media and entertainment. Social media platforms encourage users to curate idealized versions of themselves, highlighting successes while hiding struggles. Similarly, entertainment industries promote narratives that glorify superficial achievements rather than genuine character development. These influences reinforce the idea that one's worth is determined by how well they can perform or fit into societal molds.

The Consequences of Living Behind Masks

Living behind masks may provide temporary relief from feelings of inadequacy or shame, but it ultimately leads to deeper spiritual emptiness. When individuals prioritize appearances over authenticity, they distance themselves further from God's truth. This disconnect can result in anxiety, depression, and a sense of purposelessness—symptoms that reflect humanity's longing for reconciliation with its Creator.

Moreover, wearing masks prevents genuine relationships with others. True connection requires vulnerability—a willingness to be seen as we truly are—but sin fosters pride and fear that hinder such openness. As Proverbs 29:25 warns: "The fear of man bringeth a snare." When people seek approval from others instead of God, they become trapped in cycles of pretense and self-deception.

Redemption Through Christ

The good news is that redemption from this cycle is possible through Jesus Christ. While Romans 3:23 acknowledges humanity's sinful condition, it is followed by Romans 3:24-25: "Being justified freely by his grace through the redemption that is in Christ Jesus." Through His sacrificial death on the cross and resurrection, Jesus offers forgiveness for sins and restores our relationship with God.

This redemption allows believers to shed their masks and embrace their true identity as children of God (John 1:12). No longer bound by fear or shame, they can live authentically—secure in the knowledge that their worth comes not from human approval but from God's unconditional love.

Conclusion

Sin plays a significant role in shaping human behavior by driving individuals toward pretense and performance. However, understanding this dynamic through Scripture reveals both the problem and its solution. While sin separates us from God's glory and compels us to wear masks that hide our brokenness, Jesus Christ provides a way back to authenticity through His redemptive work on the cross.

As Apostle Bill Amor emphasizes throughout this book: To be born again means more than just turning away from sinful actions—it involves rejecting false identities imposed by sin and embracing one's true self in Christ. By doing so, believers can break free from cycles of performance-driven living and experience genuine transformation rooted in God's grace.

Key Scripture Reflection: "For all have sinned..." reminds us that no one is exempt from sin's influence. "...and come short..." highlights humanity's inability to meet God's standard on its own. "...of the glory of God;" points us toward reconciliation with Him through Jesus Christ—the ultimate source of truth and authenticity.

Chapter 5: Jesus Christ – The True Light

Introduction: The Light That Dispels Darkness

In a world filled with confusion, deception, and moral ambiguity, the words of Jesus in John 8:12 stand as a beacon of hope and clarity: *"Then spake Jesus again unto them, saying, I am the light of the world: he that followeth me shall not walk in darkness, but shall have the light of life."* This profound declaration reveals Jesus Christ as the ultimate source of truth and guidance. His light exposes the falsehoods perpetuated by worldly systems and illuminates the path to eternal life. In this chapter, we will explore how walking in Christ›s light reveals our true identity and empowers us to live authentically in a world that often encourages pretense.

The Nature of Christ's Light

The metaphor of light is used throughout Scripture to symbolize purity, truth, and divine revelation. In declaring Himself "the light of the world," Jesus asserts His role as the one who brings spiritual enlightenment to humanity. Just as physical light dispels darkness and reveals what is hidden, Christ's light exposes sin, deception, and falsehoods.

The Bible frequently contrasts light with darkness. Darkness represents ignorance, sin, and separation from God (Proverbs 4:19; Ephesians 5:8). Without Christ's illumination, humanity remains lost in spiritual darkness. However, when we accept Him as our Savior and follow His teachings, we are brought into His marvelous light (1 Peter 2:9).

Key Scripture Reference: *"For ye were sometimes darkness but now are ye light in the Lord: walk as children of
light."* (Ephesians 5:8)

Exposing Falsehoods Perpetuated by Worldly Systems

Worldly systems—whether through media, entertainment,
politics, or culture—often promote values that are contrary
to God's truth. These systems encourage individuals to
conform to societal norms rather than seek their identity in
Christ. They glorify materialism, self-indulgence, and super-
ficiality while downplaying virtues such as humility, integrity,
and righteousness.

Jesus' role as "the true light" (John 1:9) is critical because
He exposes these falsehoods for what they are. For example:

- **Materialism vs. Eternal Treasure:** Media often
  promotes wealth and possessions as measures of
  success. However, Jesus teaches us to store up
  treasures in heaven rather than on earth (Matthew
  6:19-21).

- **Self-Indulgence vs. Self-Denial:** Entertainment
  frequently glorifies indulgence in sinful behaviors.
  Yet Christ calls us to deny ourselves and take up our
  cross daily (Luke 9:23).

- **Superficial Identity vs. True Identity:** Social
  media fosters an environment where people curate
  idealized versions of themselves for approval from

others. In contrast, Jesus invites us to find our true identity as children of God (Galatians 3:26).

By walking in Christ's light and aligning ourselves with His Word rather than worldly influences, we can discern truth from lies.

Walking in the Light Reveals Our True Identity

One of the most transformative aspects of following Jesus is discovering who we truly are in Him. When we walk in His light:

1. **We Become Children of God:** Through faith in Christ's redemptive work on the cross, we are adopted into God's family (John 1:12). This new identity frees us from striving for approval from others.

2. **We Reflect His Glory:** As believers grow closer to Christ through prayer and studying Scripture, they begin reflecting His character—becoming «the light of the world» themselves (Matthew 5:14-16).

3. **We Are Empowered to Live Authentically:** Walking in truth liberates us from wearing masks or playing roles dictated by society. Instead of seeking validation from others or conforming to cultural expectations, we live confidently according to God's purpose for our lives.

Key Scripture Reference: *"But if we walk in the light, as he is in the light...the blood of Jesus Christ his Son cleanseth us from all sin."* (1 John 1:7)

Practical Steps for Walking in Christ's Light

To fully embrace Jesus as "the true light," believers must actively pursue a relationship with Him through:

1. **Daily Prayer:** Communicating with God allows His Spirit to guide us away from darkness.

2. **Studying Scripture:** The Bible serves as a lamp unto our feet and a guide for righteous living (Psalm 119:105).

3. **Fellowship with Other Believers:** Surrounding ourselves with fellow Christians strengthens our faith journey.

4. **Rejecting Worldly Influences:** By being discerning about what we consume through media or entertainment—and filtering it through biblical principles—we protect our minds from deception.

Conclusion: Living Out Our Faith

Jesus' declaration that He is "the light of the world" challenges every believer to examine whether they are walking fully in His illumination or still clinging to shadows cast by worldly systems. To follow Him means rejecting falsehoods that distort reality and embracing truths that lead us closer to God.

As Apostle Bill Amor emphasizes throughout this book—
media and entertainment may tempt individuals into acting
out roles that do not align with their true selves; however,
when rooted firmly within Christ's radiant truth believers can
confidently step forward unmasked unashamed authentic
reflections divine image.

Key Scripture Reference: *"Ye are all children...of day; not
night nor do you belong to the dark"* Thessalonians.

Chapter 6: Transformation Through Repentance

Repentance is one of the most profound and essential steps in the journey of spiritual rebirth. It is not merely an act of regret or sorrow for wrongdoing, but a complete turning away from sin and a deliberate decision to align oneself with God's will. The Bible consistently emphasizes repentance as a prerequisite for salvation and transformation, making it a cornerstone of the Christian faith. In this chapter, we will explore the biblical foundation of repentance, its transformative power, and how it leads to spiritual renewal.

The Call to Repentance

The call to repentance is central to the message of both the Old and New Testaments. From the prophets in ancient Israel to John the Baptist and Jesus Christ Himself, repentance has been proclaimed as necessary for reconciliation with God. Acts 3:19 declares: **"Repent ye therefore, and be converted, that your sins may be blotted out, when the times of refreshing shall come from the presence of the Lord."** This verse encapsulates the essence of repentance—it is both an acknowledgment of sin and an active turning toward God.

The Greek word for "repent" used in this passage is *meta-noeo*, which means "to change one's mind" or "to think differently afterward." This change is not superficial; it involves a deep transformation of heart and mind that results in a new way of living. Repentance requires humility, as it begins with recognizing our sinful nature and our inability to save ourselves apart from God's grace.

Understanding Sin and Its Consequences

To fully grasp the importance of repentance, we must first understand what sin is and how it separates us from God. According to Romans 3:23: **"For all have sinned and come short of the glory of God."** Sin is any thought, word, or action that goes against God›s perfect standard. It creates a barrier between humanity and God, leading to spiritual death (Romans 6:23).

Sin also distorts our identity. Instead of living as children created in God's image (Genesis 1:27), sin causes us to live according to worldly desires and selfish ambitions. This separation from God leaves us spiritually empty, searching for fulfillment in things that cannot satisfy.

Repentance addresses this brokenness by acknowledging our need for forgiveness and restoration through Jesus Christ. Without repentance, there can be no true reconciliation with God.

The Process of Repentance

Repentance involves several key steps:

1. **Recognition of Sin**
   The first step toward repentance is recognizing our

sinfulness before a holy God. Psalm 51:3 says: **"For I acknowledge my transgressions: and my sin is ever before me."** This recognition often comes through conviction by the Holy Spirit (John 16:8), who reveals areas in our lives where we have fallen short.

2. **Godly Sorrow**
True repentance involves godly sorrow—not just regret over being caught or facing consequences but genuine remorse for having offended God. As Paul writes in 2 Corinthians 7:10: **"For godly sorrow worketh repentance to salvation not to be repented of..."**

3. **Confession**
Confession is an essential part of repentance. When we confess our sins to God, we acknowledge His authority over our lives and seek His forgiveness. First John 1:9 assures us: **"If we confess our sins, he is faithful and just to forgive us our sins, and to cleanse us from all unrighteousness."**

4. **Turning Away from Sin**
Repentance requires action—it is not enough to feel sorry; we must turn away from sinful behavior entirely. Isaiah 55:7 encourages this step: **"Let the wicked forsake his way, and the unrighteous man his thoughts: and let him return unto the Lord..."**

5. **Turning Toward God**
Finally, true repentance involves turning toward God in faith and obedience. This means seeking His guidance through prayer, studying His Word, and striving to live according to His commands.

The Transformative Power of Repentance

When we repent sincerely, something miraculous happens—our sins are forgiven, our hearts are renewed, and we are reconciled with God through Jesus Christ's sacrifice on the cross (Colossians 1:21-22). Acts 3:19 promises that when we repent and turn back to God, times of refreshing will come from His presence.

This "refreshing" refers not only to spiritual renewal but also to peace with God—a peace that surpasses all understanding (Philippians 4:7). Through repentance:

- We experience freedom from guilt because Christ has paid the penalty for our sins (Romans 8:1).

- We receive a new identity as children adopted into God's family (Ephesians 1:5).

- We are empowered by the Holy Spirit to live transformed lives that reflect God's love (Galatians 5:22-23).

Living a Life of Continual Repentance

While initial repentance marks the beginning of our relationship with Christ, it does not end there. As believers grow in their faith journey, they must practice continual self-examination and repentance whenever they fall short (1 John 2:1). This ongoing process helps maintain intimacy with God while fostering spiritual growth.

Repentance should also extend beyond personal transformation—it should inspire believers to share God's message with others so they too can experience renewal through Christ.

Conclusion

Repentance is more than an emotional response; it is an intentional act that leads directly into spiritual transformation—a critical step toward being born again as described by Jesus in John 3:3-7. By turning away from sin completely while embracing God's grace wholeheartedly through faith in Jesus Christ alone—believers can experience true freedom along with eternal life promised by Him who loves them unconditionally!

Key Scripture Revisited: **"Repent ye therefore—and be converted—that your sins may be blotted out—when times-of-refreshing-shall-come-from-the-presence-of-Lord!"(Acts3;19)**

Chapter 7: Casting Off Old Roles

Key Scripture: *"...put off concerning the former conversation the old man... And that ye put on the new man, which after God is created in righteousness and true holiness."* (Ephesians 4:22-24, KJV)

Introduction: The Call to Transformation

The Apostle Paul's exhortation in Ephesians 4:22-24 is a profound call to transformation. It challenges believers to abandon their "old man"—the sinful nature and habits they once lived by—and embrace their "new man," a life renewed in Christ. This process of casting off old roles is not merely about behavioral change but about a complete renewal of identity. In this chapter, we will explore what it means to shed the roles imposed by sin, culture, and worldly influences and step into the authentic identity God has designed for us.

Understanding the "Old Man"

Paul uses the term "old man" to describe our pre-conversion self—a life dominated by sin, selfish desires, and separation from God. The "former conversation" refers to our previous way of living, shaped by deceitful lusts (Ephesians 4:22). Before coming to Christ, many of us adopt roles or personas dictated by societal expectations, personal ambitions, or even survival mechanisms. These roles often mask our true selves and keep us trapped in cycles of sin.

Characteristics of the Old Man:

1. **Corruption through Deceitful Lusts**
   The old man is corrupted by desires that promise satisfaction but ultimately lead to destruction (James 1:14-15). These could include greed, pride, envy, or addiction.

2. **Conformity to the World**
   Romans 12:2 warns against being conformed to this world. The old man thrives on societal approval and worldly success rather than seeking God's will.

3. **Spiritual Blindness**
   The old man operates in ignorance of God's truth (Ephesians 4:18), unable to see beyond temporary pleasures or achievements.

These characteristics highlight why it is essential for believers to cast off their old selves entirely.

The Roles We Play

In a world heavily influenced by media and entertainment, people often adopt roles that are not reflective of their true identity in Christ. Whether it's striving for perfection on social media, conforming to cultural stereotypes, or playing a part to gain acceptance, these roles can become prisons that prevent spiritual growth.

Examples of Common Roles:

1. **The Performer** – Someone who constantly seeks validation through achievements or appearances.

2. **The Victim** – Someone who defines themselves solely by past pain or failures.

3. **The Rebel** – Someone who rejects authority but remains enslaved by pride or anger.

4. **The People-Pleaser** – Someone who compromises their values for approval from others.

These roles may feel necessary at times but ultimately hinder us from experiencing the freedom found in Christ.

Putting Off the Old Man

Paul's instruction in Ephesians 4:22 is clear: we must actively "put off" the old man. This requires intentional effort and reliance on God's grace.

Steps to Cast Off Old Roles:

1. **Recognize Your True Identity**
   Begin by understanding that your worth comes from being a child of God (John 1:12), not from any role you play or how others perceive you.

2. **Confess and Repent**
   Acknowledge areas where you have clung to sinful

habits or false identities (1 John 1:9). Repentance is key to breaking free from these patterns.

3. **Surrender Control**
   Let go of the need to control how others see you or how your life unfolds (Proverbs 3:5-6). Trust God with your future.

4. **Renew Your Mind Through Scripture**
   Replace lies with truth by immersing yourself in God's Word (Romans 12:2). Meditate on verses that affirm your identity in Christ.

5. **Walk in Obedience**
   Commit daily to living according to God's principles rather than societal norms (Galatians 5:16).

Putting On the New Man

After casting off the old man, Paul instructs believers to "put on" the new man—a life created in righteousness and true holiness (Ephesians 4:24). This new identity reflects God's character and aligns with His purpose for our lives.

Characteristics of the New Man:

1. **Righteousness**
   Living in right standing with God through faith in Jesus Christ (Philippians 3:9).

2. **Holiness**
   Being set apart for God's purposes and walking in purity (1 Peter 1:15-16).

3. **Authenticity**
   Embracing who God created you to be without pretense or fear (Psalm 139:14).

The new man does not seek validation from worldly sources but finds fulfillment in pleasing God alone.

Living Out Your New Identity

Casting off old roles is not a one-time event but an ongoing process as we grow closer to Christ. Galatians 2:20 reminds us that our lives are no longer our own; we live through faith in Jesus who gave Himself for us.

Practical Ways to Live Authentically:

- Surround yourself with fellow believers who encourage spiritual growth (Hebrews 10:24-25).

- Serve others selflessly as an expression of your new nature (Matthew 20:28).

- Share your testimony boldly as evidence of God's transformative power (Revelation 12:11).

By living authentically as children of God, we reflect His glory and draw others toward Him.

Conclusion

Casting off old roles requires courage and humility but leads to unparalleled freedom and joy in Christ. As Paul writes in Colossians 3:10, we are being renewed daily into His image through knowledge of Him who created us anew.

Let go of every false identity today—whether imposed by sin, society, or self—and embrace your true calling as a redeemed child of God! Remember Paul's words:

"If any man be in Christ, he is a new creature..." (2 Corinthians 5:17).

Chapter 8: Renewing Your Mind Through God›s Word

The process of being born again is not a one-time event but an ongoing transformation that requires the renewal of the mind. The Bible, particularly in the King James Version (KJV), emphasizes the importance of aligning our thoughts and actions with God's truth. In this chapter, we will explore how studying scripture serves as a powerful tool for renewing the mind, enabling believers to resist worldly influences and walk in alignment with God's will.

The Importance of Renewing the Mind

The Apostle Paul writes in Romans 12:2, "And be not conformed to this world: but be ye transformed by the renewing of your mind, that ye may prove what is that good, and acceptable, and perfect, will of God." This verse underscores two critical aspects of spiritual growth: resisting conformity to worldly patterns and embracing transformation through mental renewal.

Renewing the mind involves replacing old thought patterns—those shaped by sin, culture, or media—with thoughts rooted in God's Word. It is through this process that believers can discern God's will and live lives that reflect His character.

God's Word as a Lamp

Psalm 119:105 declares, "Thy word is a lamp unto my feet,

and a light unto my path." This imagery portrays scripture as both a guide and a source of illumination. Just as a lamp provides clarity in darkness, God's Word sheds light on life's challenges and decisions. Without it, we risk stumbling through life without direction or purpose.

In today's world, where media and entertainment often promote values contrary to biblical principles, it is easy to become spiritually disoriented. However, by immersing ourselves in scripture, we gain clarity about who we are in Christ and how we should live.

The Role of Scripture in Mental Renewal

1. **Revealing Truth**
   Jesus prayed for His disciples in John 17:17, saying, "Sanctify them through thy truth: thy word is truth." The Bible reveals absolute truth about God, humanity, sin, salvation, and eternity. By meditating on scripture daily, believers can counteract the lies perpetuated by society.

2. **Transforming Thought Patterns**
   Philippians 4:8 instructs believers to focus on things that are true, honest, just, pure, lovely, and praiseworthy. Studying scripture helps us cultivate these qualities by reshaping our thought patterns to align with God's standards.

3. **Equipping for Spiritual Warfare**
   Ephesians 6:17 describes the Word of God as "the sword of the Spirit," an essential weapon for combating spiritual deception. When faced with temptations

or doubts fueled by worldly influences such as media or entertainment trends, scripture equips us to stand firm in faith.

Practical Steps for Renewing Your Mind Through Scripture

1. **Daily Reading**
   Set aside time each day to read the Bible systematically. Whether you follow a reading plan or focus on specific books or themes (e.g., Psalms for encouragement or Proverbs for wisdom), consistency is key.

2. **Meditation**
   Joshua 1:8 advises meditating on God's Word day and night so that it becomes ingrained in our hearts and minds. Reflect deeply on verses that resonate with you; consider their meaning and application.

3. **Memorization**
   Psalm 119:11 states: "Thy word have I hid in mine heart, that I might not sin against thee." Memorizing scripture enables you to recall it during moments when guidance or encouragement is needed most.

4. **Application**
   James 1:22 reminds us to be doers of the Word—not hearers only—lest we deceive ourselves. Apply biblical principles practically in your daily life by making decisions based on scriptural truths rather than cultural norms.

5. **Prayerful Study**

Before reading scripture each day ask God for understanding (Psalm 119:18). Pray over passages asking Him to reveal deeper insights into His character & purpose.

Resisting Worldly Influences

Media & entertainment often bombard individuals w/messages promoting materialism, immorality and self-centeredness. By grounding yourself firmly within framework provided bible able discern reject harmful ideologies instead embrace eternal truths.

Colossians 3:16 Let the word of Christ dwell in you richly in all wisdom, teaching and admonishing one another in psalms and hymns and spiritual songs, singing with grace in your hearts to the Lord.

Chapter 9: Walking in Truth Amidst Deception

Introduction: The Challenge of Living in a Deceptive World

In today's world, deception is pervasive. From the subtle manipulation of advertisements to the outright falsehoods propagated by media and entertainment, it can be difficult to discern what is true and authentic. As believers, we are called to live in truth, even when surrounded by lies. This chapter explores how Christians can walk in truth amidst deception by grounding themselves in God's Word, which is the ultimate source of truth.

The foundation for this chapter is found in John 17:17, where Jesus prays to the Father on behalf of His disciples: **"Sanctify them through thy truth: thy word is truth."** In this prayer, Jesus reveals that sanctification—being set apart for God's purposes—comes through embracing and living out the truth found in Scripture. This divine truth equips believers to navigate a world filled with falsehoods and remain steadfast in their faith.

Understanding Sanctification Through Truth

To understand how to walk in truth amidst deception, it is essential first to grasp what Jesus meant by "sanctify them through thy truth." Sanctification refers to the process of being made holy or set apart for God's purposes. It involves a transformation that begins at salvation and continues throughout a believer's life as they grow closer to God.

Truth, as defined by Jesus, is found in God's Word—the Bible. Unlike the shifting opinions and values of society, God's Word is unchanging and eternal. Psalm 119:160 declares, **"Thy word is true from the beginning: and every one of thy righteous judgments endureth forever."** By immersing ourselves in Scripture, we allow God›s truth to shape our thoughts, actions, and decisions.

Sanctification through truth means more than simply knowing biblical facts; it involves allowing those truths to penetrate our hearts and transform our lives. As Romans 12:2 instructs us: **"And be not conformed to this world: but be ye transformed by the renewing of your mind..."** This renewal comes from meditating on God›s Word and applying its principles daily.

The Nature of Deception

Deception has been a tool of Satan since the beginning. In Genesis 3:1-5, we see how the serpent deceived Eve by twisting God's words and appealing to her desires. This pattern continues today as Satan uses lies to lead people away from God's truth.

Modern media and entertainment often perpetuate these lies by promoting values that contradict Scripture. For example:

- Materialism is glorified as the key to happiness.

- Immorality is normalized under the guise of freedom.

- Self-centeredness is encouraged instead of selfless-ness.

These messages create a distorted view of reality that can influence even Christians if they are not vigilant. Ephesians 6:11 warns us to **"Put on the whole armour of God, that ye may be able to stand against the wiles of the devil."** One critical piece of this armor is «the belt of truth» (Ephesians 6:14), which holds everything together and enables us to stand firm against deception.

Living Authentically Through God's Word

Walking in truth requires more than recognizing deception; it demands active engagement with God's Word. Here are practical steps for living authentically amidst a deceptive culture:

1. Study Scripture Diligently

Regular Bible study helps believers discern between truth and falsehood. Acts 17:11 commends the Bereans for examining Scripture daily to verify what they were taught. Similarly, we must measure everything we hear or see against biblical principles.

2. Pray for Discernment

James 1:5 promises that God will give wisdom generously to those who ask Him. Prayer opens our hearts to receive divine guidance and strengthens our ability to recognize deception.

3. Guard Your Heart

Proverbs 4:23 advises us to **"Keep thy heart with all diligence; for out of it are the issues of life."** This means being mindful about what we consume—whether it's media content or conversations—and ensuring it aligns with God's standards.

4. Speak Truth Boldly

As followers of Christ, we are called not only to live in truth but also to share it with others. Ephesians 4:15 encourages us to speak "the truth in love," helping others see through deception without condemnation.

5. Rely on the Holy Spirit

The Holy Spirit plays a vital role in guiding believers into all truth (John 16:13). By yielding ourselves fully to His leading, we gain clarity amidst confusion and strength against temptation.

The Rewards of Walking in Truth

Choosing authenticity over pretense brings numerous spiritual benefits:

- **Freedom:** Jesus said in John 8:32, **"And ye shall know the truth, and the truth shall make you free."** Living according to God›s Word liberates us from bondage to sin and societal expectations.

- **Peace:** Isaiah 26:3 promises perfect peace for those whose minds are stayed on God because they trust Him.

- **Eternal Perspective:** Walking in truth keeps our focus on eternal realities rather than temporary distractions (Colossians 3:2).

Moreover, living authentically glorifies God by reflecting His character—a testimony that can draw others toward Him (Matthew 5:16).

Conclusion

Walking in truth amidst deception requires intentionality and reliance on God's Word as our ultimate guide. While worldly influences may seek to distort reality or lead us astray, Scripture provides an unshakable foundation upon which we can build our lives.

As Apostle Bill Amor concludes this chapter with John 17:17— **"Sanctify them through thy truth; thy word is truth"**—he reminds readers that sanctification comes not from human effort but from embracing divine revelation found only in Scripture. By committing ourselves fully to this process, we can live authentically as children of light who shine brightly even amid darkness (Philippians 2:15).

Conclusion: Walking in the Light of Christ

As we come to the end of this journey, let us reflect on the incredible truth that being born again is not just a one-time event but a lifelong transformation. Through the power of Jesus Christ, we are no longer bound by the roles and masks imposed by the world. Instead, we are called to walk in freedom, authenticity, and purpose as children of God.

The media and entertainment industries may continue to project illusions and false narratives, but as born-again believers, we have been given the light of Christ to discern truth from deception. We are no longer actors playing parts dictated by society; we are new creations (2 Corinthians 5:17), living out our God-given identities with boldness and joy.

Remember that this transformation is not something you achieve on your own—it is the work of God's Spirit within you. As Philippians 1:6 reminds us: *"Being confident of this very thing, that he which hath begun a good work in you will perform it until the day of Jesus Christ."* Trust in His faithfulness to complete what He has started in you.

Let this book serve as a reminder that your life has eternal significance. You were created for more than temporary applause or fleeting approval—you were created to glorify God and enjoy Him forever. As you continue your walk with Christ, may you grow deeper in your relationship with Him, allowing His love to transform every area of your life.

Now, let us close with a prayer:

A Prayer for Deeper Relationship with Jesus Christ

Heavenly Father,

We come before You with hearts full of gratitude for the gift of salvation through Your Son, Jesus Christ. Thank You for calling us out of darkness into Your marvelous light and giving us new life through the power of being born again.

Lord, we acknowledge that without You, we can do nothing. We ask for Your Holy Spirit to fill us afresh each day, guiding us into all truth and helping us to live lives that reflect Your glory. Teach us to walk in authenticity and humility, shedding every mask or role that does not align with who You have called us to be.

Father, help us to resist the temptations and deceptions of this world. Give us discernment to recognize falsehoods and courage to stand firm in Your truth. May our minds be continually renewed by Your Word so that we may prove what is good, acceptable, and perfect according to Your will.

Lord Jesus, draw us closer to You each day. Help us to know You more deeply—not just as our Savior but as our Friend and Shepherd who walks with us through every season of life. May our relationship with You grow richer and sweeter as we spend time in prayer, worship, and meditation on Your Word.

Finally, Father, use our lives as testimonies of Your grace and love. Let others see Christ in us so that they too might be drawn into a saving relationship with You. Empower us to be lights in this dark world—ambassadors for Your Kingdom who bring hope wherever we go.

We surrender ourselves completely into Your hands today. Have Your way in our lives and lead us ever closer to Yourself until the day we see You face-to-face.

In Jesus' mighty name we pray,

Amen.

May this prayer inspire you daily as you walk boldly in your identity as a born-again believer! Remember always: "Ye are the light of the world" (Matthew 5:14). Shine brightly for His glory!

About Apostle Bill Amor

Apostle Bill Amor's life is a testament to the power of faith, perseverance, and divine intervention. Diagnosed with autism as a child and considered high-functioning as an adult, Apostle Amor has faced challenges that would have broken many.

Born into a world that often misunderstood him, young Bill struggled with feelings of isolation and inadequacy. Despite these challenges, he displayed remarkable determination. At the age of 12, he achieved a significant milestone by winning a reading competition—an accomplishment that filled him with pride and optimism. However, this joy was short-lived when his mother tearfully shared devastating news from the doctor: he was not expected to live beyond the age of 28 to 32.

This revelation shattered his world. Overwhelmed by fear and hopelessness, Bill sought solace in his best friend John Straw, only to discover that John had been taken away by his brother Andy. Feeling abandoned and consumed by anger, he fled into the woods near his home. It was there, amidst the trees and shadows of doubt, that he cried out to God in desperation.

Bill's life changed forever on that fateful day. As he climbed a steep hill toward his neighbor's house, he encountered what can only be described as a divine vision: Jesus Christ Himself appeared before him at the top of the hill near a chain-link fence. The image was vivid—Jesus stood before him with pockmarks where His beard had been removed and glistening divots on His cheeks and chin. He did not resemble traditional depictions; instead, He appeared timeless yet distinct from modern trends.

This miraculous encounter marked the beginning of Apostle Amor's transformation. From a young boy who felt lost and unworthy, he grew into a man devoted to spreading God's message of love and repentance. Through trials and tribulations—including struggles with literacy—he found strength in faith and discovered his purpose as an apostle.

Apostle Amor's mission is clear: to guide others toward spiritual healing by sharing his testimony of divine grace. With humility born from hardship and wisdom gained through faith, he invites readers to embark on their own journeys toward repentance and renewal.